The Secret Ants Society
and
The Government Cover-up:
The Film Animation Story

Part 1 and Part 2

MR. PATRICK JACKSON

authorHOUSE®

AuthorHouse™ UK Ltd.
1663 Liberty Drive
Bloomington, IN 47403 USA
www.authorhouse.co.uk
Phone: 0800.197.4150

Published by AuthorHouse 10/21/2013

ISBN: 978-1-4918-7585-8 (sc)
ISBN: 978-1-4918-7588-9 (e)

The film animation story is about life and hardship in the United Kingdom and the struggles of people to pay their bills and feed their families. It's also about people being out of work and claiming money from the state to pay bills and keep a roof over their heads. In short, this is the result of one man's determination to stand up and fight for the good of the British people. I wanted to write a book to expose the government leaders that are making life hard for the people trying to make a living in the United Kingdom. The government industries are taking away jobs by making the country unproductive and running the economy into the ground. The government is forcing people into redundancy and unemployment by mismanaging the economy. People in high places are robbing the country. There is dishonesty and corruption at the top of the infrastructure, people paying themselves high wages without giving us a say in how to spend our money.

The robbers are taking money from the British economy, including the British working class and poor. We are under attack by a system of dishonest people who have being voted into power to manage the finances of the country and look out for our well-being. Thus far, we have not seen anyone at the top with the power to stop these people from destroying us. We need to scare this country back on course to give the British people back their dignity. The only way to do that is to root out the system that is pushing this country into bankruptcy. In my view, only by voting in a new set of people who exhibit honesty and determination will this country recover from its economic nose dive. Things will get worse for people who do not have money to look after themselves, and that includes me, Patrick Jackson. I feel that, if someone does not do something, the working class people (and other people with no jobs) will be pushed into poverty, depression, and homelessness. This could put us on the wrong side of the law, turning us into criminals because we are poor. From there, death is the only option.

I do not want to live in poverty if I know that I have a skill to offer. Others may think it is foolish to attempt to take on the very system that is pushing us all into depression, but I hope there are people in my community with the drive and determination to take on the government. I am just a one-man army with a political opinion, but if I can write a book that convinces others they are not alone, I can make a difference. If people support my attempt to take on the government (and to stand as an MP), I will be the first to show people we can succeed. And if this book and film make money, the money will go toward sponsoring this independent party and supporting the team of people that will help run it. The British People

Voting Union will be among the best candidates running for election.

If you want to take part in this project, email:
thesecretantssociety@hotmail.co.uk

Chapter 1

You may think the poor ants haven't got anything to worry about, but they have problems just like we do. They have feelings for each other. They look after each other and protect themselves from danger to the colony. And they would fight to the death to protect their family from danger.

In an ant society, all ants help to look after the baby ants from birth to adulthood. After all, they are all part of the same family. This care makes the colony stronger.

The head of the ant colony is the queen ant, and her job is to keep laying eggs so the colony can get bigger.

The queen ant is much bigger than other ants in the colony. She is so big and fat when pregnant that she needs help removing the eggs before they are hatched.

The labouring worker ants remove the eggs from the queen and take them to a safe place where they are stored before hatching into baby ants. Carer ants look after the baby ants when they hatch.

The ant colony is very organised: there are different groups of ants that do different jobs. The ant colony needs food, so a group of ants go in search of sustenance for the others. They work together as a team; if something is too big or too heavy to carry, they all pull together to bring the food back to the nest.

The security ant's job is to prevent intruders from entering the habitable space. They protect their homes (and the other ants) from attack. If the nest gets damaged, the builder ants will work hard to repair or rebuild the structure.

Scout ants look for materials to build or repair their homes, and they work as a team in order to maintain a large enough store of materials.

Architect ants do all the planning. They relocate the nest, scout out new possible locations, and help build the structure. The space always needs cleaning, so all ants take turns getting rid of anything that is not wanted.

Teacher ants are there to educate the baby ants about life to prepare them for their journeys into adulthood.

Army ants are the military force of the ant colony. They stave off threats—which are common—such as aggressive animals and rainwater.

Chapter 2

Only by looking at an ant's pure determination to work hard on a team and keep the family unit together will you be able to understand the means of building a bigger and stronger nation.

Don't let the past drag you down. Some of us focus on the past, on the damage other nations have inflicted on our people. But that resentment can be a hindrance. You must never forget the past, but you must recognise that the past won't help you in the present day.

Without education we are slaves to the system; we have to depend upon other people to give us things because we cannot make them ourselves.

It was not just a lack of education, and poverty that made people use other people as slaves. Those factors were just part of the equation. There was also a form of deception and conspiracy against the true worth of people, which was used to enslave them.

If we keep on fighting the system rather than educating ourselves, we could be setting ourselves up to be abused by others. We need to look at what we can do for our own future.

Putting our educational values ahead of our fight for history will give us the power to enter any industry, and when we are fully qualified, use those skills in any country in the world. Even without a job, skills allow us to make money.

The ant's society developed as a unit in terms of its finances, business ventures, jobs, and education. It took the good with the bad. And just as they have achieved as a nation, we can also achieve. We can make our nation proud of us and prevent others from thinking we are only one step away from being animals.

In human society, we find the upper class, the working class, and the lower class. We are organised into different groups and our background determines how successful we will become. Only our education allows us to enter any other groups.

Our qualifications can make us rich and powerful. Our education can make us leaders; it can grant us power and success. You can do anything you like and go anywhere in the world.

Human society needs leaders. It does not matter whether one works at a factory or whether one is the president of a country. If one has the ability, one can do anything. Don't let anyone tell you that you cannot succeed.

Many of us rely on others to lead us. Those people use us as free votes. They ask for our help to put them in power, but then they make us poorer and hurt the lower class.

The only way out is to work hard and do whatever jobs you can do. In short, keeping your head above water is the only way to survive hardship.

The results of the American race between the African American president and the leader of the opposition party in November of 2012 goes to show that, when people are determined to make a change in their lives, they can elect leaders capable of fighting for the best interests of the *entire* nation. Indeed, the people in America queued up for hours to vote for a man they believed in, a man they were convinced would changes their lives.

How did Obama convince the American people that he would lead well? In part, he was honest with the people. In the end, the people trusted him and voted him into power.

How can we demand the same trust and honesty from our politicians in the United Kingdom? How do we know what they say is true? The British people don't trust or believe in anything that some of the UK politicians say. Thus, when it comes time to vote, it is unfair to ask us to vote for the Labour Party, the Conservative Party, or the Liberal Democrat Party.

Whether you're an upper-, middle-, or lower-class citizen, you have important needs. All races have needs, and no matter which country you come from, you have needs. Obama looked at how he could benefit all classes of people. We require the same kind of honesty in the United Kingdom.

It's not that we don't want to vote for the established parties; rather, we expect them to be more truthful, honest, and open with the British people. Also, they should not make promises they cannot keep. We don't want politicians to use our votes to get them into power only to dump us after the election.

Some people say, "If we don't vote, we don't have a say in how the country is run." I say we should have a reasonable choice in terms of who we vote for and how that person shapes our nation. We need to vote in politicians who will put systems in place to help people. Also, we need some of our own people to become politicians.

Politicians should put skill training systems in place in the local communities to assist people out of work who need new skills to gain independence. They should provide jobs that are easier to get for those with and without qualifications. And they should increase minimum earning so the lower-class people can maintain their lives. Also, politicians should build a stable future for us; they should help us fight crime the right way without putting us under pressure to commit crimes.

We need a manifesto we can all rely on, something that will give people the confidence to vote for politicians again.

We need a voting union so we can get together as one big group of British people to show the politicians what we need and what they can do for us. We are fed up with politicians getting their own ways and making livings off our misery. There is no one to fight for the poor when our politicians let us down.

The British People Voting Union could be a way to unite and speak to politicians we might vote for. It would be great to let them know that, if they let us down, we can prevent them from being in office.

This is my way of trying to unite the British people, to speak to the politicians or government and let them know that the British voters won't put up with any more dishonesty or mismanagement.

As a nation, we have a voice. How much longer are we going to stand by and accept the situation and conditions we are faced with. As Bob Marley says, "Get up, stand up; stand up for your rights."

Chapter 3

L ow pay, high rents, and high mortgages will put you in the lowest pay range. Those conditions could lead to desperate times.

The working-class people are having a terrible time making ends meet. Some people are paid more so don't experience too much hardship, but there are other people who have very rough lives. And the low wages, high unemployment, poor education, high education costs, and lack of much paid skill training make the problem worse.

The government is responsible for the health and care of the British public. We vote these people into power to look after all our needs. We pay their wages to put systems in place that help us out when we are in need. But the government has put us in a bad situation, left us desperate to fight among ourselves.

Our people are struggling to find well-paid jobs in the workforce. They are not receiving promotions in line with the cost of living, growing family units, and outgoing expenditures. Instead, people must fend for themselves. Some people have to use alternative means to get money, and that puts some people at odds with the law.

People suffer due the existence of theft, violent crimes, mental breakdowns, prostitution, and the need to participate in medical experiments for money. The government leaders are all wealthy people; they don't understand what poverty, feels like. Therefore, they have no feelings for other people's feelings.

Our government officials promise us that things will get better, but because they don't stick to their plans, some people suffer and die due to poverty. After looking at the problems the government should be solving, I have reached the conclusion that they don't care. All that is on their minds is how to get into power, keep up appearances, apply stamps, and attain knighthood.

The system is designed to keep us under control. If we protest for a better life, the government will put systems in place to keep us quiet. The police control us; they don't protect us. Instead, the police protect the powers that be.

If you cannot meet all your bill payments, you will be sent threatening court orders. You may even go to prison if you don't have the money to pay. But maybe your wages are so low that you just cannot afford to pay. A poor person is more likely to go to prison for not paying his or her bills.

Chapter 4

If you get evicted from your home and live on the street, you can get on the wrong side of the law. Hard-working people get evicted from their homes every day. The law has been designed to hurt the lower-class people. Low wages and high unemployment have made us a target of the system.

If you're unemployed and trying to find a job—especially if you don't have marketable skills—it's hard to pay your bills. And it's frustrating when you keep applying for jobs and see that there are many people applying for the same jobs.

Have you ever heard the saying, "Crime does not pay"? I am here to tell you that crime does pay, and the government profits from it. Crime makes the government millions of pounds every year. The government depends upon people committing crimes by making us desperate.

If we were all good people, there would be no police force, no law courts, no lawyers, no lawmakers, and no prisons. Insurance companies would not need to insure our cars or houses. All those people and more would be out of a job.

So when someone throws bricks into your house, steals your goods, and tries to murder you, that person is enabling the existence of certain jobs. Likewise, when crime is high in your area, the insurance companies benefit from those crimes by raising your insurance rates.

When a crime is committed, the criminal is often given a lighter sentence so he or she can go back out there and put fear into people. In sum, the criminal creates panic, which causes people to insure their possessions.

The criminal is not asked why he or she committed the crime, or even what lead him or her to commit it. Similarly, he or she is not asked what could be done to prevent the person from engaging in criminal activity again. If you help a man change, he will change, but if you send him back out with the same circumstances, he will only do worse.

How come we have such a massive police force? Not much is done to change people who commit crimes. And where are our people getting illegal guns from to commit crimes against each other? How do they get these guns into the country, into our communities?

There is a secret world out there that only the people in high places, know about. They have a language that only they can use to back each other up.

It is no coincidence that there is high unemployment and a high crime rate among our people. I think there is a secret world of cover-ups that

11

we do not know about. Those people keep the jobless from borrowing money from banks, which pushes up the crime rate. They build fewer flats for people who need specific accommodations. They also put pressure on people to buy new homes so the estate agents and private landlords will benefit.

The government needs to make money from our misery in order to pay its workers. The government takes advantage of our ignorance, and we'll have to pay for what we do not know.

Often, when violent crime is on the increase, the public demands more police on the streets. Great happiness and celebration fill the system. The public has cried out for more police on the beat, so the government can recruit more police. Ask yourself this question, ***Do we really need more police?***

It's like a cat and mouse game: the police catch the criminals, and the system lets them go. It's a big, vicious circle. How many police officers do we need to catch the same criminal that the system keeps letting go without justifying the cause? It could be a waste of public money to keep recruiting police officers who don't get the job done.

There is a secret world out there, and the public needs transparency, not a hidden book. We would like to know why asylum seekers who enter the country are always the first on the council list for council flats. I have to think it's all part of a government plot to put pressure on the British public to buy more private homes.

There are a lot of people who cannot afford to buy their own homes. And there are also those who cannot even afford to rent private accommodations. Those people depend upon their local government authorities and their local council to provide reasonably priced rental properties.

The government allows families to live in overcrowded homes instead of making homes available for them in their communities. Where is the care for the people? This country is not just about one type of people; it is a multicultural place.

Chapter 5

Things need to happen to stop shops and restaurants from selling food products that are harmful to our health. People are living in fear of their lives every day. There are people among us who sell dangerous food and drinks. There was a documentary shown on BBC1 on 1 October 2012 about these shops. There are other similar documentaries about food that could do serious harm to our bodies. Do an Internet search to prove me wrong.

We need to set up our own businesses to stop others from trying to harm us. We should have an organisation that consists of *our* people—if other nations can do it, why can't our people?

We need inventors, designers, businessmen and businesswomen, creative people, people with motivation and stamina, and strong and determined people who are willing to work hard.

We need people who will not give up when things go wrong, people who are willing to work together, trust one another, and invest in a collaborative business.

By cooperating, we can build many businesses together. By putting some money together, we can work as a team to build businesses that our people will be willing to use. All we need to get going is a group of people willing to come together. If twenty people each put in £100 for the first month, that is £2,000 for that month. If the group keeps putting money in for five months, that works out to be £10,000 in just five months.

For example, your team could open a small takeaway food shop. You all would share the profits. You must all be willing to back each other up: if the shop needs a supply of food to sell, then you must put your finances together. If you all work together, you will all succeed in the long run. If your shops need repairing, put together a team to perform any repairs. Appoint a team leader from the group to keep things fair, sign a contract. Always hold group meetings to talk about how the shop is running. We are stronger together as a group.

The black business cooperative group is a group that invests money into new businesses. The group supports them by buying goods, carrying out repairs, and building stronger businesses. This is a new concept: putting together a group of people willing to put money into starting up a business.

Things are hard at the moment and people need jobs. This is a chance for us to work together as a team and share the profits of our work.

But what happens if someone wants to leave the group and take his or her money out of the project? We will have to replace that person after giving him or her a fair share of the profits up to that point. This will be a very profitable project, so the larger the business, the better off we'll be.

The black business cooperative group will benefit black people in many ways. If we have our own shops, our people will buy from us and support us. Our clean shops with reasonable prices will be inviting.

By inviting people to take part in setting up black businesses, we can build a bigger network and create more jobs. In the future, we can reward people who are part of the biggest and best teams. We can put on big, dancehall shows and invite people who support us.

Chapter 6

I have heard the following statement many times: "Other people are running the shops that sell the things we all buy." I have also heard people wonder how they do that. The answer is simple: they all need each other; they are a very close family group. At times, they fight among themselves, but at the end of the day, they cooperate and help each other. They constantly ask each other's advice and loan each other money to build their businesses or buy a house.

Back in the 1960s, it was hard for any immigrant to find work or an accommodation. Those people stuck together; they worked and saved their money. And up to twelve of them might share one house. Perhaps six worked night shifts and six worked day shifts. In that sort of situation, the inhabitants might share six beds.

When the immigrants got paid, they refrained from opening the wage packet. Instead, everyone living in the house gave their wage packet to the head of the house. The head of the house managed the finances and gave the others enough money to get back to work. No money was wasted.

In those days, it was hard for any immigrants to get money from the banks to buy a house, so they joined together as a team to buy one house with lots of rooms. They all lived in that big house and rented out any spare rooms to help with the bills.

The more people who lived in the house, the quicker they paid off their mortgage. Everyone who took part in paying off the mortgage would benefit. When the house was paid for, they helped each other buy another house until everyone had his or her own house. And their hardship and planning paid off.

Chapter 7

The Africans, Jamaicans, and other West Indian people had their own way of building up a group in order to survive in the 1960s. After all, they also found it very hard to borrow money from the banks. Thus, they formed a strong team of family, friends, and associates who came together to join a scheme called *pardoner.*

Finding accommodations was very hard, so most of our people only rented rooms at first. Racism was so bad in England that the only way to survive was to group together with your own people.

Many racist fights broke out in the Harlesden area (black men were targeted by racist white people). It was only by grouping together that we could fight off our enemies and build a stronger team of reliable people to finance our lifestyle. In short, by saving up and lending each other money, they made ends meet.

There were many pardoner saving schemes spread among our people in England. That was the only way to get a large amount of money, take care of outgoing bills, and bring their families abroad to England.

The Jamaican community in Harlesden got larger over time. Our people used the pardoner saving scheme to put down deposits to buy more houses. They also rented out the rooms in their houses to help pay the bills.

As a community, they put on dance shows in their homes and community halls. They also held domino tournaments and arranged coach trips to the seaside. They truly became united.

The pardoner scheme was so successful that some people did not need to borrow money from the banks. Many people formed a union of dedicated people willing to put money together. If twenty people put in £100 each per week, they would net £2,000 in one week. Everyone who put in money got £2000 over a twenty-week period. There was also a system in place for everyone to receive payments from the first to the last will collect their £2,000.

The pardoner scheme was our safety net back in the 1960s; it was like our little bank. We gave our money to a trusted person called a banker. He or she worked for the group and collected the money from each person (about £10.00 each). It's not a lot of money, but that is how the pardoner system works: all you need to do is wait your turn.

The pardoner system helped our people back in the days when they all needed help. And it was the most reliable saving system at the time.

Other groups of people have been using similar systems to help each other with finances. The Europeans have been running a banking system for many hundreds of years, and they started lending money to people in a similar way.

Chapter 8

The Black Business Cooperative Group is similar to the pardoner system: everyone who puts some money into the project and sticks to the plan of helping others can reap the benefits.

A person comes up with an idea for a business and puts together a team of dedicated people willing to support the project. It's advantageous to get rid of time-wasters who will delay the project or try to usurp authority. The person who created the project takes charge of it.

People who invest money in the project will share in the profits, even if they don't do any work. Those people are called sleeping partners. If they are putting in the same amount of money as everyone else, they should have an equal share in the profits. Thus, not everyone has to take part in the day-to-day running of the business; folks can hire someone else to do the work for them.

A small percentage will be deducted from each person's money. Those funds will be thrown back into the business to pay staff wages. If a person doesn't want any money to be deducted from his or her investment, he or she will have to help run the business.

If a project goes sour, it could be one person's fault. Thus, don't forget to sign a contract and keep records of each person's invested money. Be honest and open from the start; you may have to open a bank account to keep track of the money. Make sure any card you use to put money in doesn't have standing or handling charges.

If you cannot open a bank account because of bad credit, you can open a pay-as-you-go, prepaid credit card account. You can get top-up cards in some high-street banks, money shops, or on the Internet.

Hold a group meeting before and after recruiting people to your team. Make sure that you all agreed before you commit yourself.

We need many investors to lend a hand to build up black business throughout England. Many black businesses suffer from poor finances or an incomplete strategy. Musicians, business people, and others who have made money could invest in these new, small businesses.

Chapter 9

Our people are always talking about how other people are more successful than black people. That is because we never sat down and asked each other what we need to do to help one another build businesses. What we need is advice and assistance.

We can succeed by maintaining communication with each other, supporting each other's businesses, and promoting each other's businesses. We can print and distribute newsletters detailing all present and upcoming businesses in every community.

Business owners should make sure their businesses or shops are clean and not guilty of charging too much money for goods or services. Also, speak to one another and your children about people who are manipulating our people; teach them to work together.

We can create employment for ourselves, and that will eliminate crime in our communities. On that note, let us move away from music that encourages our people to commit crime.

Invest in our people. You will not lose; you will win all the time. How do I know this? Because I know that there are enough Jamaicans, West Indians,

Africans, and others who will support us if we use this system.

I think it would be great to rent a large work unit with, say, ten shops in one building. The people in those units could support each other. The hairdresser will have lots of customers. The sound engineer will have lots of people visiting him or her, the estate agent will be very busy, the retailer will have a constant influx of people.

It would be even better to buy such a unit. But a small group of people can open a small takeaway shop as a start. It won't take much effort—don't let the corner shops or convenient stores frighten you off.

Chapter 10

There are people among us who do things in secret. And if we learn about the groups actions we will become ill.

The people come from different parts of the nation and decide what we eat, how long we live, how clean the air is, whether it's worth spending money on things, which medicines we take, which diseases will be researched, etc.

Some of these people put things in the food products we buy, but we don't know what until it's too late. Many of us buy our food from supermarkets and think the food is good for us, but all the food in the shops—from a packet of crisps to a bottle of water—will harm us sooner or later.

Is it a coincidence that people who live in tropical countries (who grow their food and keep their farm animals free of any chemicals or pesticides) suffer from fewer diseases and live longer than we do? Also, people from the rainforest don't have the same kinds of disease we have in the West.

I am no scientist, but it would not take a genius to pick any food product sold at a shop, do an Internet search on the ingredients, and find out what you're eating. You might find that the food contains dangerous chemicals, trans fats, too much sugar, too much salt, or something else entirely.

Some food manufacturing companies are stakeholders in pharmaceutical companies that make the medicine we use to cure the illnesses caused by the food products! I wonder whether we are guinea pigs who test out their food products and help them research new medicine.

The food we eat is killing us slowly. By the time some of us reach forty years old, we will develop diabetes, high or low blood pressure, or cancer—the list is endless. The strangest thing is, they try to make you believe that *you* are the cause of your illnesses.

All food packaging should tell us which chemicals and pesticides have been used on the goods. Packaging should let us know whether the food will cause an allergic reaction, an illness, or something else nasty.

We must start buying and selling products that are naturally grown. Each product has its harvesting period. Many things in tins or frozen packages are not healthy. Fresh, organic, and pesticide-free products are the best; we need to get back to nature.

Chapter 11

Many of us buy our West Indian foods from food shops without knowing which poisons we might be ingesting. I am not exaggerating. All such shops should be properly and regularly inspected to ensure the food is safe.

More rigorous research should be conducted on dangerous chemicals that are being put into some mass-produced food products. Manufacturer's may have ulterior motives for their actions, after all, so it's necessary that the government be more vigilant. *All* food products (whether fresh or frozen, packaged or not) could be contaminated with dangerous chemicals.

As an example, a brand-name food seasoning manufacturer was investigated and found to be selling dangerous curry powder in shops throughout the nation. The investigation was outlined on the BBC *Panorama* show three years ago. This curry powder was so dangerous that the folks on *Panorama* advised the public not to use it. They asked all local shops to stop stocking and selling the product.

A BBC watchdog show also exposed the dangerous chemicals being used in bottles of vodka, including chlorine bleach. And those are just two examples of dangerous food products sold in shops. There are many more.

And what has the government done? There seem to be more and more companies seeking high profits, not high health and safety standards.

As a boy, I used to hear rumours of the horrible things shopkeepers did to the food we bought from them. I also heard about the disgusting places they stored meat, fish, and fresh food products being sold to us. To this day, they take our money and offer poor goods and services. Ask the older people, your elders, to tell you about their experiences. These practices go back to the 1960s and 70s.

Some of the takeaway food shops on high street have very poor hygiene standards. The meats used are not prepared and washed properly; sometimes they are not cooked. Often, you can still see blood and mucus in the chicken meat.

Not all of them use vegetable cooking oil to fry the food you eat. Some use an animal product called lard, which comes from pigs. It is greasy fat rendered from animals slaughtered for food. And the government has legalised this product. Similarly, Takeaway shops use the same oil over and over again on a daily basis. The oil used one day will be kept and used the next day. You can often taste the old oil and observe its darkness in your food.

Some fast-food restaurants do not wash or steam clean their shops, much less their cooking equipment. If they don't clean their shops, the food products are not being prepared properly. Also, some employees don't wear clean uniforms, cover their hair, or wear gloves when they serve your food. They are not following hygiene regulations.

We are the ones supporting these businesses. This is a bad choice, which is why we need to open our own restaurants. And there should be more government inspectors check on these takeaway shops.

We have spent endless money at banks, retailers, car rental companies, fast-food shops, butchers, cinemas, funeral parlours, hotels, travel services, etc. We have invested in all these companies and gotten nothing in return. We cannot depend upon others to meet our needs, so we must open our own businesses. Only then can we guarantee quality.

Chapter 12

How many of you women go to the hairdressers and learn that the chemicals used weaken your hair and make it fall out? Or have you used chemicals on your face or body that burned you? Maybe you've had a strong reaction to some product for hair, skin, or bath.

I don't think companies that make products for Afro-Caribbean people are properly regulated. The same is true for companies that import and export dangerous products for black people.

Anyone can become a manufacturer of skin and hair products for black people. We do not know whether any of those people have knowledge, qualifications, or experience in cosmetic skin and hair care for black people. We don't even know whether these people asked experienced scientists specialising in black cosmetics.

Our people head into shops and buy items to use on their skin or hair without knowing which chemicals are in the products or how dangerous the products are. If the label looks good or the shop assistant says it's okay, you will buy it.

We do not have our own cosmetic standards like other nations. And we foolishly stock and sell cosmetic products in our shops made by manufacturers that do not care about our health or safety. These lax regulations have harmed people who do not know that they can take action against these companies (or lack the finances to take legal action against them). Many people don't complain, so we don't know who they are.

We need our own manufacturers, people who specialise in making skin and hair care products for their own people.

Chapter 13

It's about time we set up our own organisations and stopped putting money in other people's pockets. We spend millions of pounds in various shops, giving money to people who don't care about our health and safety. We give them our money, and make their nations stronger.

There are jobs available for their people in their shops and businesses, but there aren't any spots for us. If we continue down this road, we will become weaker and more dependent upon them.

When something bad happens in our community, no one knows the details or who is responsible. There is no one to fight for us; there is no communication via radios, magazines, or newspapers.

We need to know what everyone is doing in order to support each other. We should be cautious and protective when meeting people for the first time and talk to each other when something goes wrong in our community. Whether it is council housing problems, police harassment, private landlords' high rental fees, problems with your child's education, immigrations advice, or problems associated with getting and keeping jobs, we need to communicate.

Let's talk about things that really matter to us and figure out how to fix them. It starts now. Let's trust each other and learn to unite as one. In doing so, others will learn to unite with us as we united with them.

We have a right to exist, develop, and flourish like all the other people of this country. Our children have a right to a good education and a successful career. If we cannot build a better world for our children, we will have achieved nothing.

Similarly, we need to allocate our wealth to the development of our future on this planet. We need to start planning and building. It is time for society to recognise us, and it is also time for us to recognise ourselves as the great people we are. For our own good, we have to become successful.

The Black Business Cooperative Group supports and manages this book.

This book was written by Patrick Jackson.

Management for the Black Business Cooperative Group

If you want to take part in this project, email me at blackbusinesscooperativegroup@hotmail.co.uk.

Alternatively, you may call me: 07597948392

The Film Animation Story of Life *and* *Hardship in the United Kingdom*

Part 2

Chapter One

It's a beautiful day in the ant's world: the day is sunny, and there is a cool breeze blowing through the city. There is excitement in the air—every ant is getting busy to go to the polling stations to vote in the new leader. There is a great deal of talk among many in the ant world. Ants are saying, "Who should I vote for?"; "What party should I choose?" "How will the government improve our lives?"

Great effort has gone into trying to pick the right candidates capable of doing the best job. But how do they know whether the candidate they choose will do a good job?

Each party has campaigned to tell the ant society what plans they will effect to make the ant world more efficient. Each candidate wrote out a manifesto explaining how to create more opportunities and improve the economy.

The Political Candidate Party may not stick to the manifesto that has been offered to the ants. It may be a trick to fool the ants into voting a certain way. None of the ants have ever been sure about the policies and procedures the leaders have put into place. The ants will have to look at which resources are on offer before they choose who to elect as their MP and leader.

Guidelines were developed by the ant community to enable candidates to describe their ideas, principles, values, and priorities as they relate to furthering the goals of the society. The ants have concerns: they have seen their colony becoming divided and losing its way ethically.

The colony has to choose wisely. As they head to the voting stations, some will change their minds. They must determine whether the manifesto is possible, clear, and good; is it targeting just a minority, or does it meet all of society's needs?

Chapter Two

There is hardship among the ants; there is not much work available and little money to buy food. Lots of ants will be out of work, so there won't be much money coming into the home for bills. In the ant society, life can be tough for those dependent upon leaders to guide them through life.

The word is out, election is near. The poorer ants are struggling to make ends meet. The political leaders have promised to make accommodations, health care, and jobs more available to the poorer ants. The manifestos sound very good to the poor ants struggling to survive, so they vote in a mass group. They do so happily.

The ants vote for different political parties, but at the end of the day, the candidate *you* vote for will run the ant world. But how do you know who to choose? Will the candidate help you or hurt you?

Chapter Three

There are three main political groups to choose from. They are all saying the same things and making the same promises to the poor ants. When they get into power, they will forget about and destroy the ants who voted them in.

All the ant leaders will make promises they cannot keep to trick you into voting for them. The leader who was in power before damaged the financial infrastructure so badly that new leaders will have trouble fixing it, which will make the ant world dysfunctional. The new leaders will earn high wages, cheat the system, and ensure that you die of hunger.

Each candidate strives to be better than the previous leader, and they deliver great speeches and unveiling seemingly great plans and policies. In the end, though, they forget their original party manifestos.

Chapter Four

The ant have become very desperate; they cry out for help with the hope that the problems will be fixed. There is a lack of work, high debt, and high unemployment among the ants, and the government is blaming the ants. But the government is not looking at the source of the problems because they would end up pointing straight back at themselves and their mismanagement. The government is making a large portion of the ant society poorer, and it wants to keep taking from them till they have no more to give.

How long can the ant government push the poor ants before they start to kill themselves and others?

If you die, the ant's government won't know that you have died, but spokespeople will tell the nation that there is more work available due to the dip in the population. They will keep applying pressure on you till you kill yourself or self-destruct by some other means. They are technically killing you, and the only way to survive is to keep a strong head and have faith in what you believe in.

These same politicians are paying themselves high wages and fixing wages for their friends. They lead an expensive lifestyle and have their needs met by the ant who are struggling to make ends meet.

Chapter Five

The ant society is facing the worst crisis in its history. The government cutbacks negatively impacted NHS hospitals, putting patients' lives. There are overcrowded wards and not enough doctors or nurses to cover shifts, which leads to poor care in the hospitals.

Low wages and the lack of necessary surgical equipment in some hospitals force staff members to use insufficient equipment on patients who need urgent medical treatment. Also, British pharmaceutical companies can't make medicine cheap enough for the sick and needy who depend upon certain drugs to keep them alive. The health services are purchasing cheaper medicine from foreign manufacturers for their NHS patients. Consequently, patients have to spend more money out of pocket for better medicine. This puts many people in a tough spot.

If the health service provided better medicine to all the people who were ill, there would not be such a glut of patients in hospitals and aftercare centres. Those who can afford private care and special medicine have a greater chance of recovering from an illness.

The NHS infrastructure has been stretched to a breaking point. Some of us will lose out, and people will start dying before their time because of cutbacks, lack of care, and poor facilities.

Also, staff members don't have enough funding to take care of patients. Surgeons operate on too many patients at once, yet there are too few surgeons available to operate on patients who need urgent treatments. Understaffed and overworked medical employees are putting patients' lives at risk and their careers in jeopardy.

It was only on 29 May 2013 that the following was said: "people are more likely to die in hospitals in the UK from having operation at weekends; due to the shortages of medical staffs available to take care of the patients."

Why is this the case? Why doesn't the government step in to investigate the criminals who work in the medical industry? Why are they allowed to take people's lives in this manner? If there is a staff shortage, people will die unnecessarily. That is murder.

Is it right for the people we trust to look after our health services to act in a way that harms us? Where are our government leaders when we need them?

Health services employs thousands of medical and technical professionals. Some of these employees come from abroad; some of them are not very fluent in English and struggle to speak to their patients or fully understand their peers. The NHS often recruits these people from abroad so they can pay them less.

This reality can create competition among the workers and reduce the standard of care patients should get from the NHS. Cheap, short-term labour and cheap medicine—that's the price the NHS pays for cutbacks on wages, medicine, and recruiting. With these cutbacks, they are setting a very bad precedent for the British National Health Service.

Just like hospitals, the surgery centres are overcrowded. You cannot see a doctor no matter how sick you are because there are too many patients registered at doctors' surgery centres. The doctors limit their patients to one medical condition per visit and ten minutes per patient. As compared to the time when doctors were given a certain amount of patients, we are fighting to get seen by a doctor. And people are dying due to the lack of care and attention.

Our doctors don't know us anymore, and they are jeopardising our lives to accommodate their schedules. Our health care providers have not properly looked at what sickness evolved from or its many causes and potential cures.

Patients who walk through a doctor's doors are not properly examined. The doctor just looks on his or her computer for a symptom that resembles what the patient is describing and prescribes the relevant medicine. The doctors tell the patients to come back in two weeks if the medicine does not seem to be working. If they don't come back, he or she feels good because the guess appeared to be right. But if the patients come back within two weeks, they are given the next medicine on the list. Remember: the first medicine has not left the system, so toxins pile up in the patients' bodies. And we are told not to mix certain medicines!

Our doctors need to send patients to specialists without considering the costs. They have to learn to put the people in their care first. And we must demand that doctors do not have too many patients. Remember: there are new doctors joining the medical field every day. If the present doctors are overloaded, new doctors and nurses should be hired to meet the needs of the many patients.

Why do you think our surgery centres and hospitals are so full of patients? It has been proven that medicines are provided to delay illnesses, not cure them. The majority of medicine produced by pharmaceutical companies no longer cures patients. Many people taking numerous medications are being killed slowly by the system that was set in place to heal them.

The past and present health care system has been dominated by pharmaceutical companies and their economic interests. But these new drugs don't cure or prevent illness at all; they just manage diseases. For years, antibiotics were the best thing to cure an illness, but they were curing people too quickly for the pharmaceutical companies to make any profits, so the pharmaceutical companies discouraged their use. They don't make money curing people; they make money keeping people sick. For pharmaceutical companies, managing a disease means that the patient will buy prescriptions for the rest of his or her life.

People's health is jeopardised by this new kind of medicine. Manufacturing companies, the government, and the medical practitioners all play a role in this travesty. It is dishonest, and it has already resulted in the loss of many lives. The pharmaceutical industry is not working; the companies are not spending money to provide good quality antibiotics any longer. Thus, we have expensive, poor medicine that does nothing to help us.

The media tells us that, if we eat well, we will live longer. We are encouraged to eat fruits and vegetables, but did you know that our government has authorised the sale of genetically modified food? That food is harmful to humans and helps keep us ill and taking our prescribed drugs.

Wise up, people! Take back control of your lives; we are not slaves to the system. The medical profession is working against you, so you should seek out your own medications from the land. Look for natural and healthy foods so you can keep yourself and your family in good shape and away from the crooked people in the health care industry. Eat fewer processed foods, make your own juice, and remember: not everything marketed as nutritious is good for you.

Some nursing homes are the worst places to send your loves ones. Many staff members have a bad attitude and behave cruelly towards the elderly people in their care. Some elders are harmed, over-drugged, or starved by the people whose job it is to care for them.

Abuse is on the rise, and patients have been attacked by staff members who don't take pride in their work or comply with the job's policies. We need more legitimate inspections of these homes.

Our government allows the inspection teams that keep an eye on these homes to inform the homes when they will visit the premises. That must be stopped. Otherwise, how will we catch the people or organisations taking advantage of those in their care?

We are finding that a majority of the organisations that take care of vulnerable people are cunning and untrustworthy. The government's laws are letting down the people it ought to be protecting; hence, we have a lot of corruption, a lack of decent care, unresolved deaths, and unresolved criminal damage lawsuits.

When thinking about caring for the elderly, it is sometimes wiser to keep them at home and hire helpers. It's also a good idea to set up a secure camera system inside the property to ensure that the helper is not harming your relatives. If you are unable to take care of them at home, make sure that you check out the organisation you have chosen to send them to and check on them. Remember: we all have to get old.

The school system in place in all the communities of the United Kingdom needs to be reshuffled. We have crooked headmasters and headmistresses being employed in areas filled with deprived children. Those leaders steal the income given to them to enhance the schools. Often, a school's financial records indicate that stolen money is recorded under *miscellaneous items.* And of course, no receipt for the outgoing money exists.

The school medical books are not correct, and children who are injured severely are not carried to hospital by staff members. Instead, their parents are called and asked to leave work to carry their children to hospital. No teachers like the way the hospitals are run, so children are left at risk. Students are often injured on the playground, but the injuries are covered up by certain staff members who want to be seen as competent.

Many schools misinform the education department about their conduct. Letters from parents have gone missing, and some people on the education department board of governors are friends with the heads of certain appointed schools that they oversee. Thus, those schools frequently receive preferential treatment.

A lot of children are excluded from schools because the teachers stand together and tell lies about the children to outside officials. Those who are meant to be the voice and support system of the children have let them down in secondary and primary schools.

At times, it is stated that the children are benefiting when they are not. Some heads of schools have no interest in the pupils they are teaching, and the teachers cannot complain or they will be fired.

We need more inspectors to root out all the bad workers in the workforce. Let the procedures be private; do not disclose to the workforce or organisation who made the complaint. Properly investigate, and if there is a crime to answer to, the person should be punished. Stop veiling the truth. We are living in a society with too much dishonest behaviour.

Chapter Six

The government is cutting back on building new, affordable homes to buy and rent. This is putting a lot of pressure on people with limited funds. More people are losing their jobs every month, forcing them to depend upon the government to pay their rents or mortgages, buy their food, and pay their utilities.

Private landlords are buying up as many properties as possible so they can rent them out to the poor, working-class people at a marked up rate. Many people on the dole cannot afford the deposit to pay for such rentals. Plus, some landlords do not accept anyone claiming benefits or other government payments. As a result, many people end up on the streets. Only charitable organisations keep these people alive by providing shelter and free food.

The cutbacks make it possible for the government to contribute to charity organisations that help people on the streets. The government should be doing everything it takes to provide every citizen with an accommodation, health care, and a good job. Instead, the government has raised taxes at an alarming rate, from 17.5 per cent to 22 per cent. Taxes should have been going down to compensate for low pay and a lack of jobs.

In the government's transition into recession, we have had rent, food, insurance, heating, electricity, and taxes go up. Nothing comes down. Still, we see the lives of bankers, politicians, and industrial tycoons improve massively.

The politicians try to get the working class to despise those who are poorer than they are. They make some believe many do not want to work. Ultimately, we have the right to look after our elderly, young, poor, sick, and vulnerable citizens as well as ourselves.

It is not for the government to withhold funding or medical help from those who needs it. Officials are trying to show that they are leading the country by making all people work; some people are non-workable because of their conditions, and we must put things into place to help them to live their lives as comfortably as possible. They are still paying taxes also, even if they are helped by our taxes. Many people are not just taking, as our government would have you believe.

Chapter Seven

Have you ever thought, ***Why are the British people suffering the worst financial crisis of this century?*** Could it be true that the previous government mismanaged our finances? Both the Labour Party and the Conservative Party have ruined our country. The elected representatives have not shown the strength of leadership required to keep Britain powerful so its people can compete with other countries for contracts and such.

We no longer produce in our own country. We buy everything from abroad, including pharmaceuticals and agricultural goods. We produce things such as deathtrap cars, cheap food, and cheap medicine. Therefore, everyone chooses to buy better products from abroad, which leaves us much poorer. In sum, our industries are suffering from other countries' industrial competition.

Why can't we have the same determination as other countries? Why can't we compete on the same scale to provide jobs for our people? If we do not manufacture, produce, and provide in our country, we will live in a perpetual recession.

It seems to me that it is easy for our government leaders to not try hard enough and pass the blame to the last or next person voted into power. That way, no individual person can be blamed for the mess he or she has created. And those people often end up earning a knighthood. In the meantime, the country is sinking into a terrible depression and we continue to suffer.

Chapter Eight

We are losing more work to foreign countries that challenge our industrial markets. It is easy for other countries to build or manufacture their products in Great Britain, and that is (maybe) the only stronghold we have left in that realm. When companies operate in Britain, they acquire a strong label to sell to other countries, and we get work in return.

The British people pay taxes to the government, as do foreign industries. Our country also has other means of selling industrial technology to other countries. Those sales will help us make good money so we can buy goods and sell to other countries. Sometimes, however, we need money for other things. It is not easy to find money to pay for things that help the nation, so our government often chooses to sell off parts of our industries to foreign buyers. But when there is nothing more to sell to foreign countries, the government will start to cut things back. And that creates huge problems.

In the end, the government will need money to keep the country running, and the only way to get that money is to take it from the poor.

Chapter Nine

The war on the poor people of Great Britain is unbearable. I never thought the government officials would go so low as to tell the people that the homes they have lived in for many years will become considerably more expensive. They make us pay a bedroom tax for every room that they the government thinks is a spare room in a house or flat. If the tenants cannot pay the tax for each room, they have to give up their homes and move into a smaller property in whichever area the council chooses. They disregard the elderly, disabled, and chronically sick so that they can put other people on the council waiting list into the house or flat that other tenants had to give up.

The government took this action because it has not put any building programs into place, programs needed to house over 2.5 million people on the council housing list.

Many years ago, overcrowding was illegal. You couldn't have several people sharing one room or a boy and girl between ages five and fifteen sharing one room. Now, a family of four can share a one-bedroom flat with a teenage boy and girl. This is wrong. As a united nation, we must make the government see and understand that they must fight for our rights.

The government is trying to pack as many people from the same family into the smallest rooms so they can spend less money on building new accommodations or refurbishing old properties. More and more council accommodations are being sold to private buyers.

Cutbacks that hurt the poor could cause people to have nervous breakdowns, which would send a lot of people into hospital with mental instability. And then they will be prescribed drugs to forget about what caused the situation. This influx of people could fill the hospitals with patients and provide more work for doctors, nurses, and other people that benefit from people losing their minds. The pharmaceutical companies will also benefit. And who is the biggest winner? Our government.

Why are they forcing the people into such desperate situations? And it's not the wealthy of our generation that these cutbacks are aimed at; no, it's the poor and working-class people.

Chapter Ten

The British people are eager to stir this country back onto the right path. But how easy will it be, given our elected leaders, to muster the passion, determination, and imagination to lead the country out of the recession fostered by the government? This country is diving into financial hell; the government is attacking the very people they need to help the country out of its financial woes. Our government may think that working-class and poor people are not required, but they are. You cannot run a country without these people because the country will self-destruct.

When the government is short on money to pay for things that they have invested in, they will cut back on anything that affects the poor! But how much can they take from the poor before the country goes bankrupt? They cannot keep borrowing money from the banks, and they cannot keep paying money to the banks that have invested and lost money that belongs to the people of this country. Money has to keep coming in for industry to keep our country running.

If there is not much money coming in to pay for the things we need to run the country, the government will have to borrow money from other countries. And we know what can happen to people who borrow without the ability to pay back. Quite often, creditors will send in people to demand their money back or use their leverage to buy bits of the country for themselves.

Thus, the money that is been earned in the United Kingdom is not staying here. Rather, the money is leaving our country to assist other countries while our own nation is on the verge of collapse. You will suffer whether you are at the highest or lowest point in this country's structure.

Let's work to make the United Kingdom a better place to live for those who are wealthy *and* all the other people who make up this country. Remember: the working-class and poor people pay your wages, yet your wages are higher than ours. We are the ones paying for the police force, the army, the doctors, the nurses, the teachers, and everyone else. We are the ones paying for our roads and transport systems; we even pay for the prisons. Yes, we the people who make up the United Kingdom are all in this together. So how come we are getting the short haul? How come you are making things so hard for us? Consider this: if we weren't here, you would not have a government to run. And if all the people in the United Kingdom chose not to vote in the next general election, you would not stand.

Chapter Eleven

We have grown up believing that the leaders of this country came from a wealthy background, which enabled them to top universities. And they have significant advantages over those who struggled through college due to financial strains.

If you want to run as an MP in this country, there is an exclusive club of people you have to befriend. And if you want to run your own independent party, you will need lots of money and the support of the British people. You will have to convince the Brits that what you're telling them in your manifesto is valid, and you will have to explain your policies lucidly.

Many people don't believe that it is possible for a non-white person to run this country. But things will have to change; the people running the country in their posh suits and upper-class language are doing more harm to the country and its citizens than good. And it is about time for a new breed of people to take charge.

I have seen many countries' citizens grow tired of the lies, deceit, and corruption that the government thrusts upon them. They then stood together against their parliamentary misrepresentation and overthrew their leaders. So why can't we (who see and know that our government does more harm than good) act. They have stopped listening to the British citizens, stopped working on our behalf. It is not about us anymore; they are cutting at the core of our being and thinking only of power.

If the leaders of this country do not look, listen, and meet the needs of the citizens, they are playing with fire. The politicians live in a bubble, they do not know how to commune with the people and act only when there are cameras around. We do not need actors in government; we need people who are positive, caring, genuine, and truthful.

Our government creates problems among our people and goes abroad and fixes other countries' problems. Remember: charity begins at home. Clean up your own backyard before you start to clean up someone else's. It is good to help others, but the citizens of the United Kingdom need help, too.

Chapter Twelve

Our government is very old, and the laws and ideas are old, too. Officials do not understand that the people are changing, the systems that they have in place are ancient. No one lives how they want us to live anymore; there is no love for the old, young, disabled, sick, unemployed, homeless, working class, or very poor. Our government has one law for the rich and one law for the poor. And the government, courts, special services, police, media, banking sector, and health care professionals are corrupt to the core.

There is a lot of unfairness in the United Kingdom, so we are asking that laws be changed in order to foster inclusivity and well-being among all people.

Our government avoids the truth about racial tensions in the workplace, universities, media, courts, etc. What do you think it would take for us to run our own independent party? And how could doing so benefit us? How could we put a team together of educated young people who have studied politics and are willing to give their political education the fuel to take on the government and make a difference. Let's learn to work together to give people the chance to use their skills to make money and feed their families and take care of themselves.

I believe that we can work together to achieve greatness in this country, so I am asking the people of Great Britain to join me in building a new, independent party. To give us a chance, I am willing to use the money from the sale of this book to give this new political party every opportunity to grow bigger.

If you think you have the political knowledge or good common sense to facilitate this plan (or you can help with funding this party), please get in touch so we can get the ball rolling in the right direction. If we do not stand up for what is right, we will let each other down. We must root out corruption from the top to the bottom, and we can only do that by working together.

Britain only needs one great power to protect it and its people. We do not need so many different political parties spending the finances of the country for their own benefit; we need a team of positive leaders who can and will work together for the benefit of the nation.

Our leaders and our people should answer to our queen, and our queen should provide for and take care of the people of the country she presides over. Where is her voice in all that is happening? There should be one law for all, and the law should not be hard to understand, process, or correct. Wrong is wrong; right is right. We have seen pornography in film and TV; celebrities have been allowed to get away with the most horrendous of crimes because of their wealth. When will all this end? We see statistics showing that things have improved, which is a lie: crime rules our nation.

How come our laws are not working to the benefit of our nation?

People of Great Britain, make your vote stand for the rights of our country and our fellow citizens. It is time for all of us to remove anything that's holding us apart or hindering our progress.

Chapter Thirteen

As the author of **The Secret Ants Society and The Government Cover-Up,** I am willing to sponsor young, enthusiastic people from Great Britain. I want to eliminate racial barriers and gather voices and opinions together to help make this independent party grow bigger and stronger. We need a different type of British people with fresh ideas to run this government.

We will need the approval of our queen, though, so be aware that this is a big task. But the teams put in place to run for office will have the queen's and citizens' interests at heart. Look at yourself and discern what role, qualification, or idea you have to bring to the table so that we can achieve this goal. No time-wasters, please. The situation is serious and changes need to be made so that all people are catered for in this country.

The only way this can be done is to set up our own independent party. So if you are finding life tough because of our present government, or you are finding it hard to find a job or a housing, for example, it makes sense for you to support us.

We are appealing to anyone who can help run this political party. If you are a standing politician (or someone who left his or her political party because of the unfairness it propagated) and would like to join this new, independent party, please contact us.

All those who believe in what this book is saying and know that we can make a change, please join us. This is not about us overthrowing the government or causing chaos upon the land; it's about what is right for our country and its citizens.

Chapter Fourteen

The British People Voting Union (TBPVU) is a united nation of British people that will have the opportunity to voice their opinions on how to make this new political party stronger and more able. Anyone is welcome to support or sponsor this independent party so we can elect a leader. Let us join our votes together so we can effect change in the lives of the British people.

How many times will we have to hear, "It will have to get worse to get better," or, "It's the last government's fault"? Wise up, people of Great Britain. Those words are used to drain our finances. When our government spends too much and resources are low, they punish the poor. They are chewing us up and spitting us out without any concern. Yet all is well at the top.

Remember: our present leader chose his team, to take with him into Downing Street. It was not residing government officials; it was his team. We are prepared to work with those who stand for the good of our queen, citizens, and country.

Our plan as a new, independent party is to elect a new government leader who can take Great Britain to great heights. People from around the world will see us and want to be like us because we stand for justice and peace, put our citizens' needs first, stop crime, reduce incarceration rates, improve our hospitals, tighten regulations on manufacturers, and many other wonderful things.

There is a lot we can do to correct the wrongs of the past and present, such as ending institutional racism, checking reckless and unrestrained greed, and thwarting corruption.

Chapter Fifteen

M aybe you see yourself as the next leader of our country, or maybe you see yourself as someone with enough determination and drive to make a difference in this country. Don't ever let anyone say it is not possible to become a leader, regardless of your background.

People are afraid to speak the truth about the things that matter to us as a country; they are afraid of the generation that leads with its power and wealth. We are institutionalised by the system and do not know how to fend for ourselves or cultivate our land. We depend upon things from other countries while watching our resources disintegrate. We are tricked by our banks into believing that, if we save or take out mortgages or insurance with them, we can get great returns on our investments. Please search for the truth. Our bank owners were and are slave traders. They are corrupt, and it's time for us to look at ways that we can change all these systems that are set in place to harm us. .

When our banks invest our money, we are not told about that activity. But when we look at their yearly profits and our yearly profits you will see a huge disparity. You're paying twice for your homes in mortgages, parking tickets, and other fees. The injustice has taken over our country, and it is crippling our stability. Our transport system is great, but we are charged a horrendous amount of money for our travel cards. What is going on? Does our government not see the harm it is inflicting upon its people?

It seems that all these great companies are profiting off the people's spending and savings, but nothing is going back into society. We are offered discounts at a cost: buy one get one free at a cost. Today, one shop reduces the price on a few items to make you think that you're getting a deal. But the next day, the price is higher. The shops encourage you to look around for the lowest prices, but the lowest price is only between one and five pence less. That is trickery. All supermarket and superstores are working together to con us. Their bosses and investors are the same people reaping wealth through our spending.

Why do you think our wages are kept at a minimum while the wealthiest of the wealthy are treated to more advantages?

The present government makes us look at the small print to prove they are the best leaders to take the country forward. They make up all types of lies to mislead; they tell us there's crime in our communities, but they show the ones they think will allows them to govern our nation by preying on our fears. It saddens me that we need to stand up for our own citizens' liberty.

Bosses in the workforce are getting very high wages, but those doing the hard work on the ground get paid very little. Therefore, we apply for loans and credit cards, and in doing so, we are left with massive debt that our wages cannot cover.

The British People Voting Union will definitely work for the betterment of all people. Whether you are wealthy, underprivileged, working class, sick, or healthy, we will stand up for you. Our country's name is Great Britain, so shall there be greatness for all of its occupants.

If reading this book inspired you to become a part of this great new political party, please withhold your votes from the unjust government leaders and join us. We can make our voices heard and cast votes that elicit positive changes. Contact us by telephone or email; we will then arrange a time to speak with you and gather information.

For this political party, I want strong-willed, wise people. I want people who understand that I, Patrick Jackson, will not always be by your side to see these changes come into effect. But if I cannot be there to support you all, I would like this political party to persist no matter how hard things get or what other people do to try to stop us from achieving success. No matter what may happen to me, The British People Voting Union must keep going for the sake of the poor people in our country.